GUARDIAN

ANGELS

GUARDIAN

Angels

ELIZABETH   RATISSEAU

19   99

FIRST PRINTING
PRINTED IN SINGAPORE

ISBN 1-883211-20-4

BOOK DESIGN:
SACHEVERELL DARLING
AT BLUE LANTERN STUDIO

LAUGHING ELEPHANT
PO BOX 4399
SEATTLE WASHINGTON 98104

The most beautiful thing we can experience is the mysterious.

Albert Einstein

Angel: A symbol of invisible forces, of the powers ascending and descending between the Source-of-Life and the world of phenomena.

J.E. Cirlot

There exists another, an invisible world, real as our own, it is all around us; it is peopled with angels; they travel with you and play a part in your lives.

Pope Pius XII

See, I am sending an angel ahead of you to guard you along the way and to bring you to the place I have prepared. Pay attention to him and listen to what he says…

Exodus 23: 20 - 21

…our guardian angel is to us the closest angel of heaven. An intimacy with one so benign, so powerful, so faithful, if cultivated, would pay off handsomely. It would avert those unnecessary spells of loneliness that sadden life. We simply cannot feel alone when thinking of, talking to, confiding in a companion who is always there to listen, who really cares, who all year round has no desire to take a vacation from our presence.

Valentine Long

Historically speaking, for instance, [angels] are clearly the hybrid result of an extraordinary Hebrew program of cross-breeding original Egyptian, Sumerian, Babylonian and Persian supernatural beings.

Malcolm Godwin

GUARDIAN ANGELS

Each has guardian angels before him and behind him, who watch him by God's command.

The Koran

Millions of spiritual creatures
    walk the earth
Unseen, both when we wake,
    and when we sleep:

All these with ceaseless praise
    his works behold
Both day and night.

John Milton

Every age and condition of life has its special Guardian Angels. Infants have their Guardian Angels, who preserve them from danger and guard their innocence. It has often been said that no child would attain to maturity were it not for the protection of his Guardian Angel. This statement finds support in innumerable instances of mysterious protection of little children.

Benedictine Order of Perpetual Adoration

GUARDIAN ANGELS

Ever at our side is being lived a golden life. A princely Spirit is there who sees God and enjoys the bewildering splendors of His Face.

Father Faber

So glorious, so pure, so wonderful they are, and yet they are given to be your fellow-wayfarers, charged to watch carefully over you…

Pope Pius XII

He shall give his angels charge over thee to keep thee in all thy ways. They shall bear thee up in their hands, lest thou dash thy foot against a stone.

Psalms 91: 11 - 12

God's universal providence works through secondary causes…The world of pure spirits stretches between the Divine Nature and the world of human beings; because Divine Wisdom has ordained that the higher should look after the lower, angels execute the divine plan for human salvation: they are our guardians, who free us when hindered and help to bring us home.

Saint Thomas Aquinas

GUARDIAN ANGELS

What matters is that we each have an angel, whenever it was he came into our life, who loves to be with us and even in our…lapses from grace does not lose interest. More than we realize, it is our angel who prompts in us those surprising impulses of good, flashes of enlightenment, surges of confidence, which we credit to our initiative.

Valentine Long

Safe in love and peace I sleep
Through the darkness of the night;
Guardian angels watch will keep
Till I wake in morning light.

Finnish Folk Song

GUARDIAN ANGELS

The angels keep their
   ancient places; —
Turn but a stone,
   and start a wing!
'Tis ye, 'tis your
   estrangèd faces,
That miss the many-
   splendour'd thing.

Francis Thompson

I believe we are free, within limits, and
yet there is an unseen hand, a guiding
angel, that somehow, like a submerged
propeller, drives us on.

Rabindranath Tagore

Hush! my dear, lie still and slumber,
Holy angels guard thy bed!
Heavenly blessings without number
Gently falling on thy head.

Isaac Watts

Every visible thing in this world is put in the charge of an angel.

Saint Augustine

Guardian Angels…are ever ready to shield from harm. To all whose hearts and homes are open to them, they would gladly come, bringing many blessings from on high—blessings of harmony and love.

Geoffrey Hodson

The servants of Christ are protected by invisible, rather than visible, beings. But if these guard you, they do so because they have been summoned by your prayers.

St. Ambrose

GUARDIAN ANGELS

They take different forms at the bidding of their Master, God, and thus reveal themselves to men and unveil the divine mysteries to them…

…An angel then is an intelligent essence, in perpetual motion, with freewill, incorporeal, ministering to God, having obtained by grace an immortal nature; and the creator alone knows the form and limitation of its nature.

Saint John of Damascus

Make yourself familiar with the angels and behold them frequently in spirit; for, without being seen, they are present with you.

Saint Francis de Sales

Angels exist on another plane than ours. They are not subject to the laws of time and space, and they can use matter to create forms or objects to serve their purpose.

GUARDIAN ANGELS

An angel stood and met my gaze,
Through the low doorway of my tent;
The tent is struck, the vision stays; —
I only know she came and went.

J.R. Lowell

At the age of nine he always saw, just before going to sleep, someone who looked like a child of his own age. That was accompanied by a tremendous feeling of happiness. The child was blond and was enveloped in a sort of shining lustre. After this had occurred for a couple of weeks the child said: "This can't go on any longer because now your feet are touching the ground." Then he disappeared and the boy never saw him again.

H.C. Moolenburgh

GUARDIAN ANGELS

Lord, give Thy Angels every day
Command to guide us on our way,
And bid them every evening keep
Their watch around us while we sleep.

So shall no wicked thing draw near,
To do us harm or cause us fear;
And we shall dwell, when life is past,
With Angels round Thy Throne at last.

Hymn

The many references to the guardian-ship of angels in the Old Testament find their confirmation in the New Testament. Our Lord himself gave the doctrine its final sanction. When the devil quoted to him the Psalms about the protective solicitude of angels—"lest you strike your foot against a stone"—Jesus implicitly acknowledged the truth of it.

Speaking of the innocence of children, Jesus mentions endearingly in the same breath "their angels." And this prompted St. Jerome to draw a confident conclusion. "So valuable to heaven is the dignity of the human soul," he writes, "that every member of the human race has a guardian angel from the moment the person is born."

Valentine Long

GUARDIAN ANGELS

"It is unnecessary to question me," he said, "I understand what you think. You should know that these beings are men like you were once, before God began to create you. Ask this old man one day to lead you into Infinity. Then you will see what God plans to do with you and you will learn that today you are far from completion. What would the work of the Creator be if it were all done in a day? God never rests."

The old man vanished and I awoke, lifting my gaze heavenward to see the white winged angel soaring toward the stars, his long, fair hair leaving a trail of light in the firmament.

Paul Gauguin

In the French countryside a usual greeting was: "Good morning to you, and to your companion." Some Italian families set an extra place for an angel at meals, and the birthday celebration was in honor of one's Guardian Angel, not the individual.

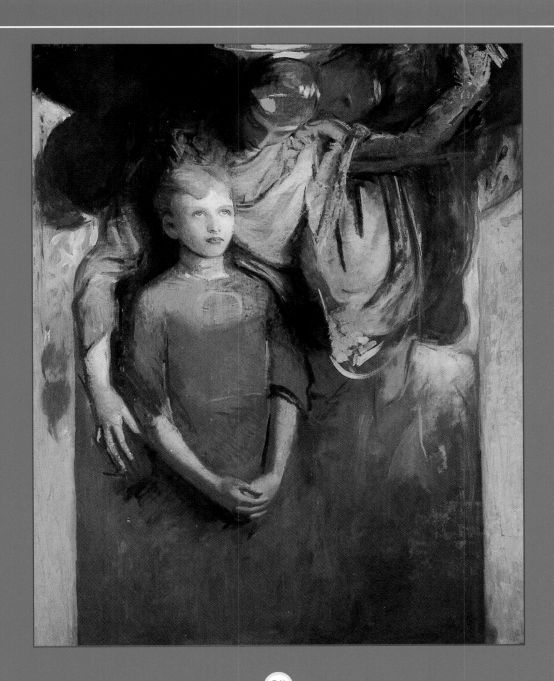

GUARDIAN ANGELS

Though impossible to accurately convey, each angelic experience reportedly has a few distinctive features. First there are feelings of peace, calm, and reassurance. Those who receive advice or direction find answers are always of a positive nature. There is a deep and lasting effect upon their lives. Those who cry for help in pain, illness, sorrow and accident are always aided in some manner, but perhaps not as they petitioned. The memory of the encounter remains clear. Sometimes people on a destructive path are shocked out of themselves and correct course dramatically and permanently.

The Guardian Angels love the homely ways of men, they desire to share the hours of labour and of ease; they love children and their play, and all the happy atmosphere of the home. They would guard men's homes, keeping away all influences of danger and of strife, of darkness and disease.

Geoffrey Hodson

Circle of circles, angels in flight, come to me and bring your light.

Prayer

lacus leonum
ubi daniel missus fuia œ abba
cue possun filli
ptun dium

GUARDIAN ANGELS

The angelic influence may act as "an odor, a scent, an emotion, a wave, a wind."

Edgar Cayce, A Reading

Angels may appear with knowledge that keeps someone from danger. They serve, in other words, as agents of God's guidance in people's lives. They remind us that God will not hesitate to communicate his will when we must know it, even if it takes rending the skies or stopping us in our daily rounds.

Timothy Jones

When man opens his heart, for even an instant, the figure he perceives (or the intuition he receives) is his Guardian Angel. When he hears the call to the spiritual life, when his psychic substance is protected from evil, when he meets certain mysterious figures in dreams, or even in waking day, who act out for him the drama of his own inner life—this is the Guardian Angel at work.

Peter Lamborn Wilson

The angels are the dispensers and administrators of the Divine beneficence toward us; they regard our safety, undertake our defense, direct our ways, and exercise a constant solicitude that no evil befall us.

John Calvin

We not only live among men, but there are airy hosts, blessed spectators, sympathetic lookers-on, that see and know and appreciate our thoughts and feelings and acts.

H.W. Beecher

There are legions of powerful angels who are assigned to help us, please us, surprise us, enlighten us. At God's Bidding, angels continuously create the environments for us to dwell in the light and splendor of God as they do.

Janice T. Connell

GUARDIAN ANGELS

The function of the angels is that of the supernatural servants of God, His agents and representatives; the Angel of Yahweh…is a manifestation of God. In old times, the *bne Elohim* and the seraphim are His court, and the angels are alike the court and the army of God; the cherubim are his throne-bearers. In his dealings with men, the angels, as their name implies, are specially His messengers, declaring His will and executing His commissions. Through them he controls nature and man. They are the guardian angels of the nations.

William Bennett

GUARDIAN ANGELS

Angels make human beings happy. It is very rare to meet someone who has met an angel who doesn't wear a smile on his or her face. To encounter an angel is to return joyful. As Aquinas says, happiness consists in apprehending something better than ourselves. Awe and wonder and the kind of power that angels represent are of such an ilk. They call us to be greater beings ourselves.

Matthew Fox & Rupert Sheldrake

We must rely on their available help. Only, the reliance is not to exclude our cooperation. People who relax every effort and expect their angels to drag them into heaven are not going to get there.

Valentine Long

And the angel said, Let me go, for the day breaketh. And Jacob said, I will not let thee go, except thou bless me.

Genesis 32: 26

GUARDIAN ANGELS

…angels appear as beings of great light. But they can appear with winglike energy fields that we discern as wings. The wings are an image that reflects the multidimensional levels on which angels operate. It's a symbol of their ability to travel through dimensions. But at their highest level they appear as light. There is nothing but light.

K. Martin-Kuri

The angels…come in different shapes and sizes, just as people do, only more so. At first you might have difficulty recognizing some of them—a voice in the suffocating smoke of a burning building; a guiding light on a stormy night; a kindly woman selling pencils—for they bear little resemblance to the popular concept of angels as serene beings with enormous wings.

Guideposts

Japanese angels may have pointed ears, a sign of spirituality in that country. Maori visions have grass skirts and shell jewelry. British angels tend to be greatly larger than those who appear in the United Sates, and they carry swords. Everywhere the helper appears in the most acceptable form, when needed most. They speak little, accomplish the aid necessary, accept no payment and vanish.

…when angels are talking with someone, they turn toward him and bond themselves to him. The bond of angel to man brings the two into a similar kind of thinking. And since a person's thought is connected to his memory, where speech comes from, the two are in command of the same language.

Further, when an angel or spirit comes to a person and is bonded to him by turning toward him, he gains entrance to his whole memory—so much so that as far as he is aware, he on his own knows everything the person knows, including languages.

Emanuel Swedenborg

So great is the power of angels in the spiritual world that, if I should make known all that I have witnessed in regard to it, it would exceed belief.

Emanuel Swedenborg

In the midst of the world crisis through which we are destined to live in the years ahead, the subject of angels will be of great comfort and inspiration to believers in God—and a challenge to unbelievers to believe.

Billy Graham

GUARDIAN ANGELS

Watch Thou, dear Lord, with those who wake, or watch, or weep tonight, and give thine angels charge over those who sleep.

Saint Augustine

As it is written, Eye hath not seen nor ear heard, neither have entered into the heart of man, the things which God hath prepared for them that love him.

I Corinthians 2: 9

This is the essence of angels—to hold on to us in our darkness and befriend us in our light.

Karen Goldman

An angel may appear to anyone, but the most touching stories of visits are those told by children who are terminally ill. These luminous and comforting visitors are so reassuring the children can assuage some of the grief of their parents, and they are able to convince other equally ill youngsters that the experience of dying is only an easy passage to a happier state. Many times suffering patients are also blessed with a remission of pain, along with the removal of fear.

They for us fight, they watch
    and duly ward,
And their bright squadrons round
    about us plant;
And all for love, and nothing
    for reward.
O! why should heavenly God to
    men have such regard?

Edmund Spenser

To our prayers they unite theirs; they inspire holy thoughts or whisper helpful inspirations...To every want of the soul through life they minister, that they may assist it to arrive safely at its journey's end.

Benedictine Order of Perpetual Adoration

Everlasting God, you have ordained and constituted in a wonderful order the ministries of angels and mortals: Mercifully grant that, as your holy angels always serve and worship you in heaven, so by your appointment they may help and defend us here on earth.

Book of Common Prayer

GUARDIAN ANGELS

The plenitude of the infinite power of God in Harmonious rhythmic measure fills all things…From it are the Godlike powers of the angelic orders; from it they have their unchangeable being and all their intellectual and immortal perpetual activities; and their own stability and unfailing aspiration to the good they have received from that infinitely good power which itself imparts to them their power and their being and their perpetual aspiration to Being, and the power to aspire to that ceaseless power.

From this ever-flowing power men and animals and plants, and the entire nature of the universe are filled; it disposes unified natures to mutual harmony and communion and gives to each individual thing the power to be according to its own particular reason and form, distinct from and unmingled with others.

Saint Augustine

How did he git thar? Angels.
He could never have walked
   in that storm.
They jest scooped down
   and toted him
To whar it was safe and warm,
And I think that saving a little child,
And bringing him to his own,
Is a derned sight better business
Than loafing around the Throne.

John Hay

PICTURE CREDITS

PICTURE CREDITS